Opening up Christianity

Christianity is a worldwide religion with many denominations, but at its heart are beliefs in God and Jesus Christ. The challenge for teachers is to portray Christianity as a living religion, relevant to young and old people in many different parts of the world.

Within this book we look at some key themes within Christianity. The importance of story is explored through learning outside the classroom with a treasure hunt. The theme of sacred text is developed for 9–11 year olds through the popular story of the Lost Son, using a graphic text, modern rewritings and the Bible as represented on the internet. Beliefs about God are diverse: work for 6–7 year olds explores five ideas that Christians have about God. Easter has been explored well in *Opening up Easter* so this book explores preparation at Lent and Advent.

For Christians, beliefs are only part of the religion; like other religions Christianity encourages action based on beliefs. The importance of caring is explored through looking after animals, using story, singing and movement. Pupils aged 7–11 enquire into the connection between what Christians believe and what they do, whether in church or in the wider community. There are opportunities for pupils to enquire into Christian practice and action using both biblical and contemporary visual sources.

For the subject leader we have provided a set of pages to improve teachers' understanding of Christianity and to support them in teaching about and from Christianity accurately and appropriately. This book is a companion to *Opening up Hinduism, Opening up Islam* and *Opening up Judaism*.

Fiona Moss

Editor

Web links: RE Today website

The RE Today website offers subscribers some free additional resources and classroom-ready materials related to this publication. Look out for the 'RE Today on the web' logo at the end of selected articles.

To access resources:

- go to the RE Today website www.retoday.org.uk

- click on the **download login** button and use the password from this term's issue of *REtoday* magazine

- click on **Primary curriculum publication – web supplement**

- click on the title of the publication and scroll down the page to find what you are looking for.

WHY DO PEOPLE TELL STORIES ABOUT JESUS?

For the teacher

In order to learn about and from Christianity our youngest children need to understand the importance to Christians of Jesus and his teaching. This unit of work shows the importance of Jesus to Christians today, even though Jesus died 2000 years ago.

The first four-page section of the book provides you with four activities that enable children 4–6 years of age to find out more about Jesus through two stories, one he told and one about him.

Our youngest children learn well through story and through memorable and meaningful events. The storytelling and active strategies in this unit should engage children and help them to remember stories so that they can share them with others.

Jesus too was a storyteller, choosing his moment to tell a story and ensuring the context was meaningful for his audience. The strategies and stories suggested in this unit are starting points: you may choose to use the strategies suggested to convey different stories told by or about Jesus.

Resources

The two stories used in this unit are found in the Bible but should be told using a more child-friendly version.

- **The Lion Storyteller Bible**
  Engaging retelling of Bible stories, ideal to stimulate you as a storyteller or to read aloud. The book comes with hints and tips on how to be a good storyteller.
  Author: Bob Hartman ISBN 9780745949802

- **Stories Jesus Told**
  Contains eight stories Jesus told including 'The Lost Coin'. Engaging and age-appropriate text and illustration.
  Author: Nick Butterworth and Mick Inkpen ISBN 9781859855881

- **Animal Tales**
  Eight stories from the life of Jesus told from the point of view of an animal. Includes the story of Zacchaeus told through the eyes of a magpie.
  Author: Nick Butterworth and Mick Inkpen ISBN 9781859856376

The following resources are available for subscribers to download from the RE Today website.
- A blank 6-piece jigsaw
- A copy of the treasure hunt clues on page 4
- A copy of the jigsaw on page 5

See: www.retoday.org.uk

What can children do as a result of this unit?

This article supports children working within the Early Learning Goals outlined below and the pupil-friendly 'I can. . .' statements for levels 1 and 2 describe what older or more able pupils may achieve through this work.

Personal, social and emotional development	show a developing respect for my own culture and beliefs and those of other people.
Communication, language and literacy	use talk to organise, sequence and clarify thinking, ideas, feelings and events; retell narratives in the correct sequence, drawing on language patterns of stories.
Creative development	use my imagination in art and design, music, dance, imaginative play, role play and stories; express and communicate my ideas, thoughts and feelings, using a widening range of methods.
Level 1	• **recognise** some stories about Jesus told by Christians • **talk about** *special people and stories in my family.*
Level 2	• **retell** stories told by Jesus and about Jesus in words, drama and pictures • *suggest a reason why Christian people tell stories about Jesus*

Activity 1 Visit from a storyteller

This unit can be presented in different ways, but creating a sense of occasion can ignite pupils' interest and engagement with the stories and ideas. Embrace your inner actor and sweep into the room as a storyteller! You may want to wear a storytelling cloak or bring a story candle or carry your bag of stories. You may of course be able to persuade someone else to take on this role.

As the storyteller, introduce the children to the person of Jesus using a series of clues from your story sack such as:

- a children's Bible
- an Advent candle
- a cross or crucifix
- a picture of a church
- a nativity tableau

Once the children have identified that they are going to hear stories about Jesus, spend time sharing what they already know about who Jesus is and for whom he is important. As a class, create a spider diagram about what they know about Jesus.

Activity 2   Zacchaeus treasure hunt

Before the session hide sets of six different objects around an area of the school grounds. At the beginning of the session organise the children into groups of six. To start the lesson each group must go and search for their six objects, place them in their group story sack and return them to the storyteller. This works best with real objects but pictures can be used instead. Depending on the area within which the hunt is being held, children could be given picture clues to help them find their clues or follow a string course through the trees.

As each group returns they need to empty out their bag and see if they can work out which story the clues might lead them to.

When all of the groups have returned, the storyteller sits the children down and tells the story of Jesus meeting Zacchaeus (Luke 19:1-10). An excellent children's version is *The Magpie's Tale* by Nick Butterworth and Mick Inkpen.

As the storyteller tells the story, the children must take the relevant object out of the bag and wave it at the storyteller.

The story of Zacchaeus can be illustrated by these six props:

- bag of money
- branch or leaves
- cup and saucer
- platform shoe
- charity collection bag
- picture of Jesus

Picture cards showing these can be found on page 4.

After sharing the story ask the children:

- How do you think Zacchaeus felt when people were being horrible to him?
- Why do you think Jesus chose to have tea with Zacchaeus?
- What can we learn from this story?
- Why do Christians still tell this story about Jesus?

Activity 3   Jigsaw stories

As the children enter the room, sit quietly counting and re - counting a set of nine pound coins. As you look up and notice the children, explain to them that you are really upset that you have lost a coin. Start looking under things and switching on the lights.

If one of the children doesn't suggest it, get the children to help you find the coin. When the coin has been found, show the children your joy – perhaps offer five minutes extra of playtime or golden time as a reward.

- Explain to the children that you are going to tell a story using a jigsaw.
- Open the box.
- Express surprise that the pieces are missing from the box.

A copy of the jigsaw can be found on page 5. This is also available as a download for subscribers.

Arrange for the children to find the pieces. You can involve all the children by making more than one copy of the jigsaw and colour coding it for each group. Once the pieces have been found, tell the story of the Lost Coin while the children put the jigsaw together.

The story can be found in Luke 15:8-10. An excellent children's version is *Ten Silver Coins* by Nick Butterworth and Mick Inkpen.

After sharing the story ask the children:

- Have you ever lost something and then found it again? How did it feel?
- Why do you think Jesus told this story?
- Can you add any more to the spider diagram?

Activity 4   Sharing the stories

Split the class into three groups. Each group must prepare a story about Jesus or that Jesus told to share with another class.

Each group will need adult support.

Two of the groups can retell the stories the children have learnt. The third group can be given or choose another story.

Each group can choose how to present the story, for example:

- treasure hunt – select pictures or objects to hide that will help to tell the story
- jigsaw – a blank template is available for subscribers to download
- picture book – a series of pictures, which the group then reads to the other class
- a series of freeze-framed tableaux photographed and shown as the story is told.

Another class is then invited into the class to learn about the stories of Jesus.

The class can finally return to their spider diagram and think about why people still tell stories about Jesus.

Perhaps invite someone in from the local Christian community to tell their favourite story and share what it means to them.

RE Today
Services

Jigsaw story: The Lost Coin

Jigsaw illustration by Bethan Moss

CHRISTIANITY IN ACTION: CARING FOR LIVING THINGS

For the teacher

This simple sequence of lessons for 5–6s uses a song, a story and a classroom 'actions' game to help children think about a Christian belief or value: the idea that God wants us to care for living things.

Children will also think about their own attitudes and behaviour towards living creatures.

The work is both active and interactive, involving:

- storytelling
- singing
- movement

These combine to explore caring and the idea that God wants people to care.

Use this work in a unit on thinking about God, or on Christian worship, or on caring and values. The work aims to enable children to think and talk for themselves about religious materials and to connect Christian belief with caring for living things. Pupils will begin to reflect on questions about God for themselves.

Links and connections

Music

Children learn to 'use their voices expressively by singing songs and speaking chants and rhymes, and explore how music is used for particular purposes', in this case to express thanks to God in Christian worship.

SEAL

Children enrich their vocabulary of emotions, thinking about 11 words that describe feelings.

Literacy

The use of story here fits well with the Literacy work on reading for understanding (in this case, listening to a story), using their ideas about character and detail.

The following resources are available for subscribers to download from the RE Today website.

W

- A PowerPoint presentation to support the story on page 9

See: www.retoday.org.uk

What can children do as a result of this unit?

The following pupil-friendly 'I can . . .' statements describe the learning that may be expected of pupils in the 5–6 age range.

Level   Description of achievement: I can. . .

1
- **talk about** the feelings in the story of Andrew and Sam
- *talk about* the idea that God wants people to care for living things.

2
- **retell** a story from experience about caring for living things
- *respond sensitively* to simple ideas about beliefs and values.

RE Today
Services

Activity 1   Learn from a Christian song

Pupils hear two versions of the song 'All Things Bright and Beautiful'. They may sing the song too. They learn that Christians believe God made all the beautiful things in the world and Christians try to be thankful to God for the earth and its beauty. Teachers can find many versions of this song recorded, or free on YouTube, for example:

See: www.youtube.com/watch?v=yZq8ZUE6GTU

A version of 'All Things Bright and Beautiful' with a simple picture sequence.

You could also use Hayley Westenra's version using John Rutter's tune:

See: www.youtube.com/watch?v=EoyvKgVywT4&
   feature=related

- After hearing two versions, ask the children to talk to a partner about which one they liked best and why.
- Listen to some reasons and have a vote.
  o who might sing this song?
  o why?
  o where?
- Do they agree with the singer that God made all the beautiful things in the world, including birds, animals, mountains, rivers, flowers, and so on?

What are their favourites of all these natural wonders?

- Put some of the words of the song on the whiteboard and tell the children it was written over 150 years ago in 1848 by a lady called Mrs Alexander.
- Ask the children which of these beautiful things they like best, and why:
  o Great creatures: elephants, bears, camels, horses, tigers
  o Small creatures: cats, dogs, rabbits, guinea pigs, foxes
  o Flowers: daffodils, tulips, roses, daisies, water lilies
  o Birds: blackbirds, parrots, sparrows, ducks, swans
  o Sights: mountains, rivers, sunsets, rainbows, stars
  o Weather: windy, sunny, rainy, lightning, clouds
  o Fruits: strawberries, apples, mangos, bananas, oranges.

- All things bright and beautiful,
- All creatures great and small,
- All things wise and wonderful,
- The Lord God made them all.

- Each little flower that opens,
- Each little bird that sings,
- He made their glowing colours,
- He made their tiny wings.

- The purple headed mountain,
- The river running by,
- The sunset and the morning,
- That brightens up the sky.

- The cold wind in the winter,
- The pleasant summer sun,
- The ripe fruits in the garden,
- He made them every one.

Activity 2   A story about guinea pigs

- Read pupils the story on page 9 about two boys caring for pets. There is a PowerPoint presentation for subscribers to download from the RE Today website.
- **Identify** and **discuss** 11 emotions and 5 ways to show caring in the story.
- **Ask pupils to** think about their own ways of showing care – to people and to animals.
- The story includes 11 emotions, and the follow-up work asks pupils to think of a time when they felt one or more of these 11 emotions.
- Put the 11 emotions on cards in front of groups of children, or the class as a whole, and ask them to choose a word and put it into a sentence about themselves:
  o I felt puzzled when . . .
  o I am interested in . . .
  o I feel special if . . . and so on.

There are 11 feelings in the story: Give these words to pupils in pairs, and ask them to put them in order while they are listening. The right order is:

> Really pleased
>
> Jealous
>
> Interested
>
> Special
>
> Cross
>
> Excited
>
> Scared
>
> Relieved
>
> Puzzled
>
> Thrilled
>
> Proud

RE Today Services

Activity 3   Chanting and movement based on the story

Pupils join in with some simple chanting and develop a movement activity to show their ideas about feelings and about caring for people and animals. They are asked to think about whether they want to thank God for some of the things they care for, and whether they want to thank other people.

* Set up the classroom as for circle time, sitting on the floor or on chairs.

* Begin with some rhythm: teacher claps hands on knees and then claps hands together in a four beat pattern. On the claps, use a sentence with four words: 'I care about pets/children/boys/girls/kindness/ fairness/sharing.' You could put some of the names of children in the class into the chant.

* Ask children to chant back to you on the claps, with enough time to remember what to do in between – too fast is impossible.

* Ask the children if they would like to lead the chant by sharing what they care about.

* Create some chants about the Christian values they have learned: 'Jesus said be kind / Jesus said show you care / Jesus said love the world / Jesus said don't fight.'

* Remind the pupils of the story of Andrew and Sam and the guinea pigs (page 9). Split them in two groups and ask one side to chant 'Care for guinea pigs' and the other half to reply with the six ways that Sam showed he cared: give them fresh food / give them a drink / let them run out / fresh straw for a bed / give them a cuddle / clean out their poos (the last one is fun, because it has poos in it!).

* Ask the pupils to think about how Andrew showed that he cared.

* Ask the class to think about how they show they care for their pets or for people they love.

* Do some more chanting in which any child can lead with a line about caring: 'tidy up my toys / give dad a hug / feed Spot my dog / play with baby Darren.'

Activity 4   My own ideas about caring

To finish the work – and to collect some evidence of what the children can do – remind the children that Christians think it matters to care, and also believe that God cares for us. They can draw four pictures of caring:

I care for . . .	To show I care, I do this:
To show I care, I do this:	**The Bible says: 'Be kind to each other' and 'God cares for you.' My picture about why caring matters:**

RE Today
Services

Caring for Liquorice and Toffee

Andrew was really pleased that Sam lived next door, because they were best friends. They weren't in the same class at school because Sam was a bit older, but they went to the same church. When he went into Sam's garden to play, Andrew sometimes felt jealous because of Sam's guinea pigs. There were two of them. One had smooth dark grey hair, and the other had patches of white and toffee coloured fur. Andrew asked 'What are they called?' 'Toffee and Liquorice,' said Sam. 'I bet you can't guess which one is which.' They laughed. Liquorice and Toffee lived in a wooden hutch on the grass, and they could come out to play in a run, which had a little door to close at night. Andrew was interested when the guinea pigs came out: they would eat a dandelion leaf from your hand, or sit on your lap, which made you feel special.

'Please can we have some guinea pigs?' Andrew asked his mum. But she always said 'You're too young to take care of them. It would end up with me having to look after them.' Dad said the same – it seemed to Andrew as if they were ganging up on him to stop him from having a pet of his own. He was cross.

At the end of term, it was the summer holiday. Sam and his mum and dad were going away for a week. They asked Andrew if he would care for Toffee and Liquorice. Andrew was quite excited. Mum went with him every day, but he did it all himself. He gave the guinea pigs some water in their little bottle. He put fresh food in their bowl. He opened the door for them to run out onto the grass. He put fresh straw in their bedding box. He even had to brush out the little brown poos the guinea pigs had done, and put them in the dustbin. It was a bit smelly. Mum watched him, smiling. The best bit was picking up the two little creatures and petting them for a few minutes. They liked to be held, and talked to: they would eat some grass or leaves from his fingers.

But on Thursday morning, when he was taking them out of the hutch, naughty Toffee hopped out of his hands and scampered away. Andrew felt scared and in a panic! 'Mum, help!' he shouted. That made the guinea pig run under the hutch. Mum got a leaf, and held it out gently to Toffee. When the little creature began to nibble the leaf, she scooped him up and put him back in the hutch. Andrew was so relieved.

When Sam got back after his week's holiday, he came round and said thanks to Andrew – he brought him a bag of sweets, and they went to play football. Andrew invited Sam to his birthday party because it was nearly 12th August, Andrew's big day – his 7th birthday. He woke up early, and he was a bit puzzled when he went downstairs, because there was no sign of a present from his mum and dad. But when he opened the curtains, he was thrilled: on the gravel in the back yard was a hutch – and inside, a small black furry guinea pig! He ran upstairs and woke his mum yelling: 'Is it for me? Is it for me?' She laughed and laughed as they went downstairs to see the guinea pig together. 'I'm going to call him Fluff,' said Andrew. 'I wonder why!' replied Mum.

'I wonder why you bought me a guinea pig?' Andrew said. 'Well,' Mum replied, 'it was really because when Sam was away you showed me that you are able to care for a creature in so many different ways.' They took Fluff out of his hutch, being careful not to let him scamper off. He was the best present! Andrew felt proud.

There is a fun PowerPoint presentation sequence to go with this.

See: www.retoday.org.uk

WHAT DO CHRISTIANS SAY GOD IS LIKE?

For the teacher

RE is a demanding subject to teach to younger pupils because the concepts are difficult and the questions are uncertain. The subject looks at beliefs, which are varied, and so teachers need to be relaxed about saying 'I don't know' or (even better) 'That's a great question, Carly. Does anyone else have an answer for it, or a thought about it?' The temptation to duck the issue when children ask big questions is strong, but good teachers are brave and self-aware enough to resist!

This work approaches the question of beliefs about God. The method uses the motto 'hard concepts are learned through simple activities'. The activities used here are

- card sorting
- thinking
- talking in pairs
- choosing an image.

The concept of God is as diverse as the number of human beings on the planet; this makes it too difficult to handle all at once. This work requires looking at five things Christians say about God, inviting children to respond to these ideas simply.

If you think for a moment about the essential core knowledge of RE, then thinking about Christian understandings of God would surely be part of it. God is the key idea in the UK's and the globe's largest religion: Christianity. Those are good reasons to tackle this topic with 6–7s. Another is that they are rather interested in God-talk.

What can children do as a result of this unit?

The following pupil-friendly 'I can . . .' statements describe the learning that may be expected of pupils in the 6–7 age range.

Level	Description of achievement: I can. . .
1	• **use religious words** like 'belief', 'God and 'Jesus'
	• **recognise** one thing Christians believe about God
	• *talk about God and about their own feelings and ideas.*
2	• **identify** two or more ideas about God that Christians believe
	• *recognise how difficult some questions about God are to answer*
	• *respond sensitively to questions about God for themselves.*
3	• **describe** two different things Christians believe about God
	• *use a metaphor to express an idea about God for themselves*
	• *make links between Christian beliefs and their own ideas.*

Curriculum links

This work has some good connections to Literacy, where in Year 2 pupils begin to see how metaphors can make writing interesting, and in their poetry they look at patterns on the page.

The 'kenning' poem used in this unit is a good example of poem patterns in two-word lines.

RE Today subscribers can also download the following from the RE Today website:

- A PowerPoint presentation to support Activity 2

RE Today
Services

Three activities to enable understanding about God: big ideas and big questions

Activity 1   Different roles

The teacher can begin by explaining some of his/her own roles – as teacher, son or daughter, parent, friend, and so on. Children like to hear about their teachers' lives beyond the classroom.

- Ask the children to think about the different roles they have, for example as:
  - son/daughter
  - pupil
  - sister/brother
  - friend
  - granddaughter/grandson
  - team member (e.g. in sport, clubs, games, class)

- Ask them to say two things they do in each role. Some things we do as a son or daughter (give a kiss? have a cuddle?) we don't do as a pupil. Other things we do as a pupil (put hand up to speak? ask before going to the toilet?) we don't do when we are being a granddaughter or grandson. Some things we do as a team member, but not as a friend. Gather some examples, and praise the children who give them.

- Tell the children that Christians believe God does lots of different things. Can they make some suggestions about what they think God does (some may say 'nothing')?

- Can the class make a list of ten or more ideas?

Who?

Time starter
Space maker
Earth shaper

Mud modeller
Garden planter
Fruit grower

Stable sleeper
Miracle maker
Eye opener

Cross carrier
Devil crusher
Grave buster

Promise keeper
Hand holder
Heart warmer

Cheerer upper
Energy booster
Life giver

Activity 2   Using a poem to learn what Christians think God does

Tell the children that Christians believe God has lots of different roles. Use the 'kenning' poem in the box above to start this work.

- Read the kenning poem to the pupils, and ask them what or who they think it is about.

The poem actually has two three-line stanzas each about God the Father, Jesus and the Holy Spirit, so it is a simple way to help children think about Christian ideas about God.

Put the lines of the poem on the whiteboard. There is a visual presentation for subscribers to download from the RE Today website to enable you to do this, or you can make a big copy on some cards to use in circle time.

- Ask the pupils if they can see why each line is something to do with what Christians say about God.

- Are there any lines they don't understand? Maybe someone else in the class can explain? Maybe the teacher can?

- Ask the children to take one line (i.e. two words!) of the poem each, and draw a picture to show what it means.

Activity 3 Cards and metaphors: five ideas about God

Use a cut-out version of page 13 for this activity. Copy the page enough times to use it in a group of three or four pupils – 8 or 10 sets for the class. Cut it into 15 cards and put them in an envelope.

- To begin with, tell the children that the cards are made up of five lots of three: can they sort them out into the right order? Talk about the five different sets of cards.

- Next ask the children which ones they think are the best ideas about God, and why. Talk about their favourites.

- Third, ask the pupils to make up some more 'God is like . . .' sentences for themselves, and draw pictures to go with them. Share these round the class – you could have a vote on the very best (while praising all the ideas of course!) The template below shows the children how to do it:

Teach the class that Christians believe in God the Father, God the Son (Jesus) and God the Holy Spirit. Ask them if they would like to ask any question about God, and get your TA to type all the questions onto the whiteboard. Perhaps a Christian visitor to school, or a member of your staff, would like to talk about some of the questions, or maybe other children can give their ideas to answer them.

God is like . . .	My picture:	My reason: Both are . . .

RE Today
Services

Match up: What is God like?

We asked some older Christian children aged 10 'What is God like?' They had lots of ideas. Here are five of them.

- Can you match an idea with a picture?
- Can you match them with a reason?

God is like a tree		**Big and strong**
God is like my mum		**Cares for you**
God is like a light		**Shows you the way**
God is like your shadow		**Always with you**
God is like a jigsaw		**Puzzling**

Images © Focus Multimedia, used under licence.

RE Today Services

13

WHY DO CHRISTIANS . . . ?

For the teacher

This series of activities is devised to demonstrate the connection between what Christians believe and what they do, whether in church or in the wider community. There are opportunities for pupils to enquire into Christian practice and action using both biblical and contemporary visual sources. Opportunities to stimulate more able pupils with a challenging final discussion are included.

The visual stimulus on pages 16–17 gives a window into four different churches and the practices that might be seen in the buildings: worship through singing, sharing the peace with church members, reading the Bible, listening to a sermon, taking communion and praying. The community noticeboard shows examples of the type of activities many Christians choose to spend their time supporting. While we have suggested a series of activities using this stimulus there are other ways this rich image can be used to enquire into Christian belief and practice.

There is an adaptation of this work for younger children on page 19.

See also

The following websites provide additional materials which may supplement the teaching of this unit and inform the teacher about variety of practice within and between denominations.

1 **RE Quest**
   www.request.org.uk
   A range of short videos showing worship in a variety of churches can be seen on this site. There are also examples of Christian community work with different organisations.

2 **BBC Class clips**
   www.bbc.co.uk/learningzone/clips
   Clip 4155: Sung worship in an Evangelical church
   Clip 4458: Communion in a Catholic church

3 **Glossary of terms**
   http://anglican.org/vocabindex.html
   This glossary provided by the Anglican Church offers explanations of many of the practices seen in Christian worship.

4 **Teacher information**
   www.reonline.org.uk
   The subject knowledge section of this has a chapter on Christian practice with links to other suitable websites. The teacher resource section provides other website links to extend this work.

What can children do as a result of this unit?

The following pupil-friendly 'I can . . .' statements describe the learning that may be expected of pupils in the 7–11 age range.

Level	Description of achievement: I can. . .
2	• **ask questions about** different aspects of Christian practice and belief
	• **identify** three things that might happen in a Christian church and suggest a reason why they might be important to a Christian
	• *recognise some Christian values shown by things done in the church and the community.*
3	• **describe, using appropriate religious vocabulary**, what Christians do in church and suggest why they might take part in these activities
	• *make a link between a piece of Bible text and the action of a Christian person.*
4	• **describe and link up** examples of Christian worship and Christian action
	• *suggest reasons, using a biblical quote, why a Christian might choose to support a particular community activity.*

Information file

Christian practice varies within and between denominations. The examples of Christian practice shown in the picture on pages 16–17 are found in most but not all denominations. A denomination is a branch or part of the Christian Church, including: Church of England (Anglican), Roman Catholic, Baptist, Methodist, Religious Society of Friends, Salvation Army, Orthodox.

The following resources are available for subscribers to download from the RE Today website. **W**

• A colour copy of the picture on pages 16–17

• An A4 black and white copy of the picture on page 19

• A copy of the Bible quotes resource sheet on page 18

• A colour copy of the four windows needed for Activity 2 on page 15.

See: www.retoday.org.uk

RE Today
Services

Activity 1 Looking very carefully

This activity familiarises the pupils with a picture in which a series of Christian practices are seen by looking through four different church windows. It also allows them to look closely at the community noticeboard which shows Christians in action in the imaginary community of Yawtown.

There are strong links to visual learning and pupils need to interpret what they are seeing, Pupils should be encouraged to discuss what they think they have seen with other members of their group and use previous knowledge about Christianity to support them in their observations and drawing.

Organise the class into groups of four pupils numbered 1–4 and give each group some felt-tip pens and a piece of flipchart paper.

Ask the pupils to

- Take turns: Number One comes to look at the picture from pages 16–17 (a blow-up to double size might be useful) for 10 seconds.

- Number One returns to the group and draws as much as s/he can of the picture from memory.

- When they are ready the group send Number Two to come and look, again for 10 seconds, and take over the drawing.

Over 15 minutes and six to seven visits to the picture, different groups of pupils create a picture similar to the one they are all looking at. The teacher can praise the efforts of all groups in this impossible task – which is very good at making the picture memorable.

Now move onto Activity 2.

Activity 2
Enquiring into Christian practice

Cut out each of the four windows from the picture on pages 16–17. A colour copy of the whole picture is available for download by RE Today subscribers. The individual windows are also available for download.

Stick each of the windows into the centre of a piece of A3 paper.

Arrange your class into four groups. You may want to use smaller groups in which case you will need to have two copies of each of the windows.

Each group starts off with one of the pre-prepared A3 pieces of paper. The papers are then moved in a carousel, with each group doing the new activity with a new window, building on the work of the last group.

Ask pupils to:

a **Write** any questions you have about what you can see in the window. Allow about two minutes for this. Move the paper to the next group.

b **Add in** any further **questions** and **answer any questions** posed by the first group. Allow about five minutes for this. Move the paper to the next group.

c **Research** in books or on the internet to **clarify** what is happening in the picture and then as a group write a paragraph which could be displayed next to the window to explain what is happening. Allow about 30 minutes for this. Move the paper to the last group.

d Receive the finished work and read it through. Choose two people in your picture and **draw** a thought cloud. Write what they might be thinking.

Share the finished pieces with the whole class. What has been learnt about Christian practice?

Now move onto Activity 3.

Activity 3 Belief and behaviour – so what?

This activity helps pupils to make links between Christian teaching, belief and practice and the behaviour of Christians. Christianity is about both belief and behaviour.

Arrange pupils to work in pairs. Each pair needs an A4 colour or black and white copy of pages 16–17 and a cut-up set of the Bible quotes from page 18. A black and white outline of the picture is available to enlarge on page 19.

Ask pupils to

- Take each of the Bible quotes and try to **identify** somewhere in the picture where this teaching is being followed.

- Choose five of the Bible quotes to work with and for each quote **respond** to these three sentence starters:

  Christians are taught . . .

  This means they should . . .

  An example of this being acted out in Yawtown is . . .

RE Today
Services

Love must be sincere. Hate what is evil; cling to what is good. Be devoted to one another in love.

Romans 12:9

Live in harmony with one another. Do not be proud, but be willing to associate with people of low position.

Romans 12:16

I will sing to the LORD all my life; I will sing praise to my God as long as I live.

Psalm 104:33

Give thanks to the LORD Almighty, for the LORD is good; his love endures forever.

Jeremiah 33

And don't forget to do good and to share with those in need. These are the sacrifices that please God.

Hebrews 13:16

The love of money is the root of all evil.

1 Timothy 6:10

For I was hungry and you gave me something to eat, I was thirsty and you gave me something to drink, I was a stranger and you invited me in, I needed clothes and you clothed me, I was sick and you looked after me, I was in prison and you came to visit me.

Matthew 25:35-6

And let us consider how we may spur one another on toward love and good deeds, not giving up meeting but encouraging one another.

Hebrews 10:24-6

Jesus said 'Whenever you eat bread and drink wine, remember me.'

1 Corinthians 11:26

Rise in the presence of the aged, show respect for the elderly and revere your God. I am the Lord.

Leviticus 19:32

May God our Father give you grace and peace.

Ephesians 1:2

Your word is a lamp to guide my feet and a light for my path.

Psalm 119:105

RE Today
Services

Activity 4 What would Christians do? What would you do?

This final activity allows the pupils to consider why people might want to support the different activities displayed on the community noticeboard.

As a class

- **Look carefully** at the community noticeboard. What projects can you see advertised?

- **Discuss** what each of the projects might be about.

Ask pupils to work in pairs

- **Decide** which project would you like to offer to help at or raise money for.

- **Discuss** which activity a group of 9–10 year old Christians would support. Why would they choose to support it? What Christian teaching would encourage them to support it? How would they support it?

- **Write a note** from the children to an imaginary project leader **explaining** why they want to help out with the project. Use at least one of the quotes in your note.

A final task to challenge the most able

Have a group discussion to answer the question: Is a church that only worships God and doesn't help people better than a church that only helps people and doesn't spend time worshipping God?

Making this work accessible for 5–7s

Predicting

- Give each pupil a church window outline and ask them to **draw a picture** of what they think they might see if they peeped through a church window on a Sunday morning.

- **Discuss** their drawing and then show them the picture on pages 16–17 and see what extra things might happen in a church that they haven't noticed.

Observing

- As a class, list 10 things that are being advertised on the Yawtown noticeboard.

- **Discuss** what these things are and who they might help.

- Do the pupils know of any activities like this?

Linking

'And don't forget to do good and share with those in need . . .'

Hebrews 13:16

Christians read the Bible to learn about what they believe and how they should live their lives. Share the quote with the children and ask them to freeze-frame an activity that would show Christians following this teaching.

Illustration by Sophie Hardwicke

PREPARING TO CELEBRATE: LENT AND ADVENT

For the teacher

Lent and Advent can be overlooked, or be just 'mentioned in passing'. Yet for Christians each is an important time of spiritual preparation for the greater event to come. The activities here provide practical ways for pupils to develop their understanding and to reflect on the importance of Lent and Advent for Christians today.

Activity 1 focuses on Lent, and uses a powerfully drawn presentation to engage pupils with the story of Jesus' temptation in the desert, its significance for Jesus and for Christians today.

Activity 2 focuses on Advent, the key people whose stories are remembered, and the Advent wreath. Making the wreath and unpacking its symbolism provides an engaging way of understanding the meaning and importance of Advent.

Activity 3 draws on a set of 36 cards each with a statement about Lent or Advent. Completing a variety of sorting tasks enables pupils to clarify their thinking and generate their own questions.

Activities 4 and 5 suggest ways in which the thoughts of Christians can be brought directly into the classroom – via a class blog or Twitter account, and not least by inviting a local Christian into the class.

What can children do as a result of this unit?

The following pupil-friendly 'I can . . .' statements describe the learning that may be expected of pupils in the 7–9 age range.

Level   Description of achievement: I can. . .

2
- **use religious words** to talk about what some Christians do during Lent or Advent
- *ask lots of questions about Lent or Advent and look for some answers.*

3
- **identify and describe** some things Christians believe and do during Lent or Advent
- *respond meaningfully to the idea of reflecting on events in the life of Jesus showing that I understand the impact the life of Jesus has on Christians.*

4
- **use the right words** to show that I understand things some Christians believe and do during Lent or Advent
- *show that I understand how Lent or Advent prepare Christians for the festivals that follow them.*

Information file

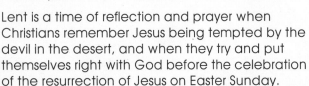

- **Lent**
- Lent is the period of six weeks (40 days excluding Sundays) leading up to Easter. Lent starts on Ash Wednesday and ends with Holy Week. Easter is the most important festival for Christians.
- Lent is a time of reflection and prayer when Christians remember Jesus being tempted by the devil in the desert, and when they try and put themselves right with God before the celebration of the resurrection of Jesus on Easter Sunday.
- **The following websites are useful:**
- **BBC Schools:**
  http://tinyurl.com/4ug5rag
- **Church of England**
  http://tinyurl.com/6e3u3cb
- **Christian Aid**
  http://tinyurl.com/3dlfpr7

Information file

- **Advent**
- Advent is the period of four weeks leading up to Christmas. It is a time of expectant waiting, hope and preparation for the birth of Jesus.
- **The following websites are useful:**
- **The Archbishop of Canterbury**
  http://tinyurl.com/6j8289r

  The 10-minute video reflection by the Archbishop of Canterbury will provide the teacher with a clear understanding of the nature and purpose of Advent and so support their discussions with children.
- **The Voice Institute**
  www.cresourcei.org/cyadvent.html

  This website describes in detail the variety of Advent customs, particularly the Advent wreath.

RE Today Services

Activity 1 Telling the story – Lent

Lent is based on the time in Jesus' life when he went into the desert for 40 days to pray and think about his ministry. There he was tempted. This story is told in the Bible in Matthew 4:1-11 and also in Luke 4:1-13.

- **Show pupils** the Lenten Reflection drawn by the Christian artist Si Smith and, as a class, create a feelings graph charting Jesus' emotions during the 40 days.

  See: www.youtube.com/watch?v=cgnBX3N3NtQ

- **Explain** that Si Smith has based his reflection on the story from the Bible, and **read** the story with the children. How well do they think Si has captured the details and mood of this Bible story? What would they change?

- Ask pupils to **suggest** what they think Christians today might do during the 40 days of Lent to help them think about what happened to Jesus and what they can learn from it.

- Pupils **complete Activity 3** to check their suggestions and develop further their understanding of the meaning of Lent.

© Victoria Beech 2011

Activity 2 Telling the story - Advent

During Advent the importance of John the Baptist, Mary and the Wise Men (Magi) in the nativity story is remembered. An Advent wreath is widely used by Christians to help focus on the stories of these key players, and this activity suggests ways of using this symbol in the classroom.

- **Make an Advent wreath** with the class - all you need is some evergreens and five candles (three blue or purple, one pink or rose, and one white), as shown in the picture below.

- **Tell the pupils** that Christians believe that the wreath is saying something very important about God, Jesus and the world. Ask them to suggest:

  o What do the evergreens represent?

  o Why is the wreath circular in shape?

  o Which candle is most important and how do you know? Who might it represent? What does it say about that person?

  o Why are each of the candles in the picture shown here a different length?

  o Explain that the candles are lit, one in each week of Advent in this order – purple, purple, pink, purple. The white candle is lit last, on Christmas Day.

- **Explain** that the pink or rose candle symbolises joy, and that in some churches the blue or purple candles represent John the Baptist (Luke 1), Mary (Luke 1–2) and the Wise Men (Matthew 3). The evergreens are a symbol of rebirth and new life.

For details of the symbolism of the Advent wreath: **See:** www.cresourcei.org/cyadvent.html

- **Tell pupils the stories** associated with each of these people and ask them how they think each person helped 'prepare the way' for Jesus.

- **Ask pupils** to suggest what they think Christians today do during Advent, as they light the candles, but at other times too during the four weeks of Advent.

- **Pupils complete Activity 3** to check their suggestions and develop their understanding of Advent.

Activity 3   Card sorting activity

Make enough sets of the 36 cards on pages 23 and 24 for each pair or small group of pupils in your class. Laminating the pages before cutting them up gives them a longer life, and copying each set onto different coloured card makes sorting them out at the end of the activity easier.

Ask pupils to:

- **Sort** their cards into three piles – those that are only about Lent, those that are only about Advent, and those that could be relevant to either. Encourage them to justify their choices to their group.

- **Feed back** their findings to the class and check for accuracy (a quick guide for the teacher is below).

- **Take** the cards for either Lent or Advent, and those in the 'either' pile. Sort them into those that are about the Bible story and those that are about what a Christian might do today.

- **Choose** the five cards that they think are the most important and which capture the 'essence' of Lent or Advent for Christians.

Pupils **move on to Activity 4 and/or 5** to check out their ideas and develop further their understanding of the meaning of Lent or Advent.

Quick reference guide

The 36 numbered cards for this activity fall into the following five categories:

1 Cards about Lent:

1, 2, 5, 6, 12, 13, 15, 18, 22, 24, 25

2 Cards about Advent:

1, 10, 11, 20, 24, 30, 33, 36

3 Cards about Lent or Advent:

3, 4, 7, 8, 9, 24

4 Cards referring to the biblical story:

9, 13, 18, 25

5 Cards about what individual Christians might do during Lent and Advent:

3, 4, 5, 6, 7, 8, 10, 13, 14, 16, 17, 19, 21, 22, 23, 26, 27, 28, 29, 30, 31, 32, 34, 35, 36

Activity 4   Blogs and tweets

Class blogs and Twitter are excellent ways of bringing into the RE classroom a variety of perspectives from all over the world to stimulate discussion and deepen understanding.

- Talk to the colleagues in your school who blog and tweet (it may be you!). Ask them to post a simple question about Lent or Advent on the school blog, ideally devised by your class, e.g. 'What special things do you do during Lent?'

- Raise awareness of the blog via a class Twitter account.

- Let pupils log on from time to time during the day to see the responses as they are received. A reply such as 'During Lent I tried to spend more time with my sister because she is having a hard time' can do a lot to generate relevant discussion – is Lent about giving things up – or about doing more?

Activity 5   Visitors in the classroom

Activities 1–4 will have provided pupils with opportunity to identify plenty of questions of their own about Lent and Advent.

A visit from a member of the local Christian community to the classroom provides an ideal opportunity for pupils to ask their questions and so consolidate their learning.

The visitor should be made aware of the preparatory activities the class are undertaking, and might be invited to contribute to the class blog or tweets as part of their preparation for the visit.

RE Today Services

Understanding Advent and Lent

1 Getting ready – preparation	**2** 40 days	**3** Passing on a smile
4 Doing a chore for someone	**5** Having a pancake party	**6** Missing a meal and praying instead
7 Reading the Bible more	**8** Watching the news and praying about what is shown	**9** Jesus
10 Making a special wreath with four coloured candles	**11** Buying a special calendar showing 24 days	**12** Sadness
13 Being tempted	**14** Saying something nice about someone behind their back	**15** The time before Christianity's most important festival
16 Making up with someone you have fallen out with	**17** Giving time generously to others	**18** Satan

19 Giving to charity	20 A period of four weeks	21 Saying sorry to someone
22 Buying or making some Easter cards	23 Talking to someone rather than texting or emailing	24 Saying sorry to God
25 Remembering when Jesus went into the desert	26 Talking with someone from a different religion or culture	27 Praying more often than usual
28 Giving some things up for a while	29 Remembering Jesus' parents	30 Buying or making some Christmas cards
31 Being generous to others	32 Going to church more often than usual	33 Remembering the birth of Jesus
34 Saying thank you to someone	35 Sharing a meal with someone	36 Attending a carol service

RE Today
Services

How and why is the Bible important for Christians today?

For the teacher

This unit explores how Christians use the Bible today and reflects on why it is important in their lives. It is aimed at 9–11 year olds.

The Bible plays a central role in the Christian faith and in the lives of many Christians around the world.

There is no single way in which the Bible is viewed by Christians. For some, the Bible is a cultural text with some valuable wisdom that might be helpful in their lives. For others, this collection of books is inspired by God and gives clear but demanding instructions on how to live. For some, the Bible is read in church on a Sunday and its general ethical approach affects their own morality, but it plays little direct role in their everyday lives. For others, daily Bible reading is an essential part of their Christian way of living. But this is an ancient text, written over many generations, some of it more than 2000 years ago – how is it that it is seen as a living authority by Christians today? This unit examines some of the ways the Bible is used as a relevant contemporary text.

What can children do as a result of this unit?

The following pupil-friendly 'I can . . .' statements describe the learning that may be expected of pupils in the 9–11 age range.

Level	Description of achievement: I can. . .
3	• **describe** two ways in which Christians use the Bible and give one reason why it is important in their lives • *make a link* between my own life and the importance of forgiveness in Jesus' teaching about the Lost Son.
4	• **identify similarities and differences** between ways in which Christians use the Bible and how it affects their lives • *apply the ideas* of being sorry, being angry, being jealous and forgiving from the story to my own life and saying if I have anything to learn from the story.
5	• **suggest reasons** why Christians interpret and apply the Bible differently, by examining the story of the Lost Son. • *explain* how and why the Bible might inspire some people, expressing my own views on whether this ancient text is relevant today.

Activity 1   Disentangling the text

Most Christians don't read ancient Hebrew and Greek. They think the Bible is important because it tells them how God wants them to live, so they need it translated into a form that they can understand.

The story of The Lost Son from Luke chapter 15 in two translations is on page 27. The translations have been tangled up to provide a disentangling task for pupils.

Disentangling

• Give copies of the page to pairs of pupils, along with two coloured pencils.

• Ask pupils to read the story carefully and underline the different translations in different colours. (Try and leave it to the pupils to identify that one is old – the Wycliffe Bible of c.1400. The other – in modern American English – is from *The Message*, published in 2002.)

Translating

• Ask pupils to have a go at translating the fifteenth-century language into modern English.

When the pupils have done this, read them the full *The Message* translation and see how close they have come. The full texts of both translations can be found at www.biblegateway.com .

RE Today subscribers can find the answers on the RE Today website.   **w**

> **NB** The Message *translation says the younger brother has wasted his living on whores (v30). This is what Jesus says, and most translations include this, or a similar term. Please be aware of this, so you can decide if you want to face that discussion with your pupils at this stage. The term has been avoided in this unit.*

Analysing

Afterwards, talk about:

• What are the differences between the translations?

• Which is easier to read and why?

• Why do Christians make new translations?

• Can you think of any possible problems with using translations of such ancient texts? For example, what happens when you don't know what a word means, such as *grutched, nighed, wroth.*

Activity 2 Interpreting a Bible story

Christians don't think Jesus told the story of The Lost Son just because it was a good story. They believe he had something important to teach his followers.

Acting it out

- Ask pupils to act out or prepare a reading of a section of the story from Luke 15.
- They need to consider the emotions and attitudes revealed at each point in the story, from the point of view of each of the main characters (e.g. father, older brother and younger brother; selfish, greedy, hopeful, trusting, foolish, resentful, despairing, sad, forgiving, joyful, loving, foolish, courageous, jealous, humble, repentant, angry, etc.)
- Where is the turning point for each character?

Interpreting the story

- Ask pupils what they think the message of the story is. What is it teaching Jesus' followers?

Note that the context at the start is very important – the teachers of the law are complaining that Jesus is mixing with sinners. Note also that the other two stories Jesus tells just before The Lost Son (The Lost Sheep and The Lost Coin, Luke 15: 3-10) describe there being 'rejoicing in heaven over one sinner who repents'.

- Give pupils the selection of meanings from page 28. In groups, get them to decide which ones are the most likely messages for Christians from the story.

Evaluating the story

Not everyone agrees exactly about the meaning for today, but generally most Christians agree that the father represents God, the younger son represents all people/sinners and the older brother represents people who already have a relationship with God. Christians believe God (like the father) is willing to forgive even the worst sinners, if they are truly sorry. Some say it should be called 'The Story of the Forgiving Father'.

- Talk with pupils about whether they think the father should have accepted his son back.

Applying the story

- Ask pupils to reply to the 'agony aunt' letter below.
- First they should do it as if written by a Christian, using the messages of Jesus' story from above, to help them with their advice.
- Second, answer it from their own viewpoint.

Activity 3 Getting the message across

Most Christians think that it is important that their children grow up to learn about the life and teachings of Jesus. Most Christian parents want their children to follow Jesus for themselves, so they find ways to try and get the message of Jesus across to them.

a Ask pupils to read page 29 which gives a page from the *Lion Graphic Bible* and compare it with the story they have read already.

- What is left out?
- Is anything added?

b Look online at the Action Bible
See: http://theactionbible.com/

It gives sample pages, including the story of the Lost Son:
See: http://tinyurl.com/6kop38p

Compare these graphic versions with an animated version, e.g.

- line-drawn animation:
See: http://tinyurl.com/6ff5ak8

- Stop-go animation from a Sunday School class
See: http://tinyurl.com/6beptrv

- Lego animation
See: http://tinyurl.com/5ury4mm

c Ask pupils to decide which of the different presentations is most effective in communicating the message of the story to children today.

- Do they tell the story accurately?
- Why is this important for Christians?

d Allow pupils to choose how to present the next four frames or next two scenes of the story. They might draw their ideas, or act them out, or animate them, or write a rap or a song or set up a shadow puppet theatre, or write a poem.

- What happens next in the story of The Lost Son?

Now go on to Activity 4

Please note this activity requires pupils to be able to access the internet to view some resources.

Dear Aunt Antonia

My best friend recently went off and broke off our friendship. Sam started saying all kinds of nasty things about me to these new friends. It really hurt. Anyway, Sam has come back and said sorry now. I don't know what to do. It's hard to forget.

Yours sincerely

J

RE Today
Services

The Parable of The Lost Son: tangled translations

Here are two translations of Jesus' story of The Lost Son. Unfortunately they have become all tangled up.

Luke 15

¹ By this time a lot of men and women of doubtful reputation were hanging around Jesus, listening intently.

² And the Pharisees and scribes grutched, saying, 'For this man receiveth sinful men, and eateth with them'.

³ And Jesus spake to them this parable, and said: ¹¹ 'A man had two sons.

¹² The younger said to his father, "Father, I want right now what's coming to me [after you die]."
So the father divided the property between them.

¹³ And not after many days, when all things were gathered together, the younger son went forth in pilgrimage into a far country; and there he wasted his substance in riotous living.

¹⁴ After he had gone through all his money, there was a bad famine all through that country and he began to hurt.

¹⁵ He signed on with a citizen there who assigned him to his fields to slop the pigs.

¹⁶ And he coveted to fill his womb of the pods that the hogs ate, and no man gave to him.

¹⁷ And he turned again to himself, and said, "How many hired men in my father's house have plenty of loaves; and forsooth I perish here in hunger.

¹⁸ I'm going back to my father. I'll say to him, 'Father, I've sinned against God, I've sinned before you; ¹⁹ I don't deserve to be called your son. Take me on as a hired worker.'"

²⁰ He got right up and went home to his father.
When he was still a long way off, his father saw him. His heart pounding, he ran out, embraced him, and kissed him.

²¹ And the son said to him, "Father, I have sinned against heaven, and before thee; and now I am not worthy to be called thy son."

²² But the father wasn't listening. He was calling to the servants, "Quick. Bring a clean set of clothes and dress him. Put the family ring on his finger and sandals on his feet.

²³ And bring ye a fat calf, and slay ye, and eat we, and make we feast.

²⁴ My son is here – given up for dead and now alive! Given up for lost and now found!" And they began to have a wonderful time.

²⁵ But his elder son was in the field; and when he came, and nighed to the house, he heard a symphony and a crowd.

²⁶ Calling over one of the houseboys, he asked what was going on. ²⁷ He told him, "Your brother came home. Your father has ordered a feast – barbecued beef! – because he has him home safe and sound."

²⁸ And [the brother] was wroth, and would not come in. Therefore his father went out, and began to pray him.

²⁹ The son said, "Look how many years I've stayed here serving you, never giving you one moment of grief, but have you ever thrown a party for me and my friends?

³⁰ But after that this thy son, that hath devoured his substance with women, came, thou hast slain to him a fat calf."

³¹ And he said to him, "Son, thou art evermore with me, and all my things be thine.

³² But this is a wonderful time, and we had to celebrate. This brother of yours was dead, and he's alive! He was lost, and he's found!"'

Interpreting the story of The Lost Son

Christians believe that Jesus told this story to teach some important lessons for his followers. Here are a few ideas.

Cut up the boxes and decide together:

• which lessons are most likely to be what Jesus wants his followers to understand

• which ones are probably not what he had in mind.

Then decide which you think are the top two most important lessons Jesus wants Christians to follow.

It's great to party and waste your money, as long as you say sorry in the end.	It is great to party and celebrate when someone turns to God.	Younger brothers are a pain. They always get to do the good stuff.
God is like the father in the story. He lets his son go his own way but rejoices when the son returns. The story should really be called 'The Forgiving Father'.	Always save your money for a rainy day. You never know when disaster may strike.	The Lost Son can return to his father at any point. The same is true for Christians. Even when they sin and go away from God, he wants them to say sorry, and he is looking out for their return.
We should always be prepared to forgive others, even when they have hurt us a lot.	The older brother represents people who already have a relationship with God, like those who are with Jesus when he tells the story. They should be pleased that God forgives sinners, not grumpy about it.	Forgiveness is crazy. Some people just don't deserve to be forgiven. The older brother is right.

RE Today
Services

The Lion Graphic Bible: The Lost Son

How do Christians use the Bible and what difference does it make?
An enquiry

THERE WAS ONCE A MAN WHO HAD TWO SONS. THE YOUNGER SAID, 'FATHER, I CAN'T WAIT UNTIL YOU'RE DEAD. GIVE ME MY SHARE OF YOUR PROPERTY *NOW!*'

'AND SO, WHILE THE ELDER SON WORKED HARD FOR HIS FATHER EVERY DAY AS HE'D ALWAYS DONE, THE YOUNGER SON SOLD THE LAND HE HAD INHERITED.

'ALL HE WANTED WAS THE MONEY, AND AS SOON AS HE GOT HIS HANDS ON IT, HE SET OFF FOR THE BIG CITY, WITHOUT A SECOND THOUGHT FOR THE LIFE HE'D LEFT BEHIND...

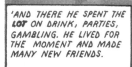

'AND THERE HE SPENT THE *LOT* ON DRINK, PARTIES, GAMBLING. HE LIVED FOR THE MOMENT AND MADE MANY NEW FRIENDS.

'BUT IT DIDN'T LAST. THE MONEY RAN OUT, AND HIS NEW "FRIENDS" DROPPED HIM AS QUICKLY AS THEY HAD TAKEN HIM UP.

'HE WAS LEFT WITH NOTHING.

'IN DESPERATION HE TOOK A JOB LOOKING AFTER PIGS, AND WAS FORCED TO EAT THEIR FOOD JUST TO SURVIVE.

WHAT ARE YOU LOOKING AT?

'EVENTUALLY HE CAME TO HIS SENSES AND REALIZED HE HAD TO RETURN HOME.

'HIS FATHER SAW HIM IN THE DISTANCE AND, FULL OF COMPASSION, RAN TO MEET HIM.

FATHER, FORGIVE ME. I AM NO LONGER WORTHY TO BE CALLED YOUR SON. PLEASE TAKE ME BACK - LET ME WORK AS ONE OF YOUR SERVANTS.

NONSENSE! THIS IS A TIME FOR CELEBRATION - LET'S FEAST! I WANT EVERYONE TO KNOW THE GOOD NEWS.

HOW CAN YOU *DO* THIS? HE'S TREATED YOU LIKE A *FOOL*! NOT *ONCE* HAVE YOU HAD A PARTY FOR *ME*, AND I'VE SERVED YOU *FAITHFULLY*!

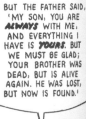

BUT THE FATHER SAID, 'MY SON, YOU ARE *ALWAYS* WITH ME, AND EVERYTHING I HAVE IS *YOURS*. BUT WE MUST BE GLAD; YOUR BROTHER WAS DEAD, BUT IS ALIVE AGAIN. HE WAS LOST, BUT NOW IS FOUND.'

Activity 4   How do Christians use the Bible today and what difference does it make?

a Christians use the Bible in different ways. Give pupils the four case studies below. Ask them to find out which of the resources listed below might be most helpful for each individual and why.

Case studies

Elly is 14. She likes to study the Bible on her own. She wants to read a passage and see what God's word has to say about the things that puzzle her about life.	Anna is a student. She isn't studying theology but is interested in languages. She wants to be able to compare different translations of the Bible and work out what all the words mean.
Jonathan is a youth leader at a church. He wants to read the Bible every day and also needs ideas for explaining the message to the 10–14 year olds in his church. He likes to watch and listen to lots of styles of music, talk and video.	Joel is 12. He is trying to read through the whole Bible in a year. He is finding it difficult but his friend has bet him £5 that he can't do it!

Resources

Logos app for iPhone http://www.logos.com/mobile/iphone	Have a look at this site Christians use for reading the Bible: http://www.wordlive.org/Home/145653.id Choose alt.wordLive
Bible+1 app http://tinyurl.com/5wplac6	Have a look at this description of Bible notes for children and young people: http://tinyurl.com/3jlr4yo

b Lots of Christians were asked, 'How has the Bible changed your life?' They had to give a one-sentence answer starting with 'Now I . . .'
Below are some of their replies. **See also:** http://tinyurl.com/6l9aemt

- Ask pupils to choose five of these statements and add another sentence to each:
  'This means that I will . . .' What are they actually going to *do* now?
  Think about the impact of the Bible on these people's everyday lives.
  Further images can be found on a Facebook gallery, some of which you may like to use in the classroom:
  See: http://tinyurl.com/3sajpex

Now I am caring, listening and helping.	Now I want to share the Bible with others.	Now I know my place in the real story.	Now I know more about God.	Now I see things more clearly.
Now I'm focused on what matters.	Now I have a guide and encouragement for daily living.	Now I have a worldview that makes sense.	Now I see how God loves me!!!	Now I can know God and find peace.

c Talk with pupils about the following statement. Ask them to come up with their answers, showing that they know that people have different ideas about it.

'The Bible is out of date and useless for anyone in today's world.' Do you agree?

Using their work from sections **a** and **b** above, and using at least one sentence starter from each of the columns below, ask pupils to put together an answer:

Some people don't read the Bible because . . .	Some Christians use the Bible every day to...	The Bible teaches that . . .	I wonder . . .
The Bible is written in different languages, so Christians . . . today because . . .	Other Christians use the Bible to . . .	Many people follow the Bible's teachings today because . . .	Even people who are not Christians might learn from the story of The Lost Son that . . .
Some Christians think . . .	Some think that the Bible is . . .	Some Christians find the Bible helpful because . . .	I think that . . .
The Bible is an ancient text but . . .	The Bible is important for Christians because . . .	Some stories in the Bible are helpful/not helpful because . . .	I agree/disagree because . . .

RE Today Services

REPRESENTING CHRISTIANITY: TEN TIPS FOR TEACHERS

In general

1 Ensure that Christianity is taught as a **worldwide religion**, choosing resources and examples carefully to reflect the variety of expression of Christian life around the world, but present in each classroom too. Help them to understand how beliefs and practices can vary, and to appreciate the richness of such diversity.

2 Give children the opportunity to learn about **what Christians actually believe** – not just about the externals such as buildings and festivals. Help them to engage with the real core of the Christian faith as it is lived out around the world today, avoiding assumptions and stereotypes, and aiming for authenticity and reality.

3 Provide regular opportunities for children to **visit places of worship**, and other places of significance to Christians. **Invite members of the local Christian community** in to RE lessons to contribute to children's learning.

4 Resources

Choosing good resources to support effective teaching of Christianity isn't always easy. The following key points will help you navigate to those that will support effective teaching and learning. Some excellent sites are suggested in Tip 10.

Books and printed resources

- Look for those that avoid the assumption that readers come from a Christian background.

- Make sure that some of the modern-day groups that might be in your class (e.g. evangelical tradition) are included.

- As well as reference to externals (e.g. festivals, buildings) look for those which have sufficient about Christian core beliefs (e.g. about the nature and role of Jesus).

- Choose those that present a positive picture of Christianity as having a place in British society and Christianity as a worldwide religion.

Websites

- Look for sites that support the educational aims of the syllabus you are teaching (e.g. an American church Sunday School site is unlikely to appropriately support school RE in the UK).

- Choose those that are free from bias, accurate and up to date, and which represent contemporary living Christianity.

For further guidance on choosing resources for RE **See**: www.natre.org.uk/rg.

5 Artefacts and visual images to have in school

Over time, build up your own collection of artefacts and visual images. Here is a starting point:

Artefacts

- different types of cross (e.g. plain, crucifix, South American)
- witness pin
- rosary beads (Roman Catholicism)
- chalice and paten
- various kinds of candle (e.g. plain, baptismal, Easter)
- nativity sets (from different cultures)
- icons (e.g. Greek, Russian)
- Salvation Army tambourine and flag
- Bible (various translations)

Visual images

- depictions of the crucifixion (classic and modern)
- Christian buildings from around the world
- Christians living in different cultures
- the Pope (Roman Catholicism)
- the Archbishop of Canterbury (Anglicanism)
- Archbishop Desmond Tutu

6 Beliefs: Jesus

The person of Jesus is central to all Christian belief and worship. Jesus is both a historical figure and a person of religious significance.

Key features in Jesus' life:

- birth and childhood; baptism and temptations; call of disciples and continuing relationship with them; teaching through parables, miracles, the beatitudes and the great commandment; Holy Week (Palm Sunday to burial); resurrection, ascension and second coming.

Jesus and his teachings are expressed through:

- lives of Christians through the ages and today; worship, festivals, rituals and celebrations; how Jesus is portrayed in the arts; how belief in Jesus has influenced cultures and ways of life.

7 Beliefs: the Bible

The Bible is a collection of 66 books. The canon (list) of books chosen for inclusion was decided in 397 CE (Common Era). There are two sections:

- **The Old Testament** (39 books) – written over a period of some 1000 years, this section includes laws, myths, poetry, songs, prophecies, history and stories.

- **The New Testament** (27 books) – covering the period from the appearance of Jesus to the deaths of Peter and Paul in 64 CE, there are four types of literature: letters (epistles), gospels, history and prophecy.

All Christians refer to the Bible and regard it as a source of authority, but within different traditions or denominations there is a variety of ways in which it is read, understood and followed.

8 Beliefs: the Christian year

The Christian year begins with the first Sunday of Advent (the fourth Sunday before 25 December). The church has set out a cycle by which all the main events in the life of Jesus and the saints are thought about.

The most important festivals for Christians are: **Easter, Pentecost** and **Christmas**.

While the details of how Christians around the world celebrate these festivals may vary considerably, there are likely to be **some common features:** reading of and reflection on the festival story; special services and acts of devotion; symbols and artefacts; social events within the church community.

9 Beliefs: denominations within Christianity

Over the course of history Christianity has broken up into a number of different churches or denominations. **There are three broad groups:**

- **The Orthodox Church** – mainly found in Eastern Europe, Russia and the Eastern Mediterranean.

- **The Roman Catholic Church** – found in all parts of the world, and accounting for some 60 per cent of all Christians.

- **The Protestant Churches** – established as a result of the Reformation, and including the Church of England, Baptists, Methodists, Salvation Army, Quakers and Presbyterians.

10 Useful websites

1 BBC Learning Zone Clips Library
www.bbc.co.uk/learningzone/clips

2 RE:Quest
www.request.org.uk

3 RE:jesus
http://rejesus.co.uk

4 REonline
www.reonline.org.uk

5 BBC Schools
www.bbc.co.uk/schools/religion/christianity

6 BBC Religion
www.bbc.co.uk/religion/religions/christianity

RE Today
Services